Worldwide
Creativity
Mindfulness

# About the Author

Worldwide Creativity Mindfulness is a family business born out of the desire to help children develop, giving them the opportunity to know themselves, to practice the art of positive affirmations, and to offer them personal development activities. We strongly believe that it is very important for children to grow up in a healthy environment, considering the fact that what we think we become, what we feel we attract, and what we imagine we create.

Reach out to us if you want to receive more free self-development materials for your children and also if you want to get notified about new releases. Also, feel free to follow us on Instagram and Facebook to find out about our Giveaways to come.

Visit our website:
www.worldwide-creativity.com

Instagram:
https://instagram.com/worldwidecreativitypress

Facebook:
https://facebook.com/worldwidecreativitypress

# Free Goodies

## HELLO PARENTS!

If you would like to receive our top 5 activities that can improve your children's life quality and also help them become stronger, grateful, and confident, send us an email with the text
**"Mindfulness Activities"** at:

# contact@worldwide-creativity.com

Worldwide Creativity
Mindfulness

# Our Growth Mindset Collection Books for kids

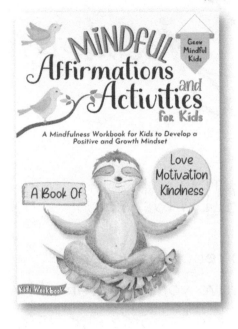

Change your child's mind-set in just a few minutes a day with the help of "Mindful Affirmations and Activities". This book contains three chapters that help children to manage their emotions, grow strong and confident. Mindful Affirmations, Mindful Coloring and Mindful Activities.

www.worldwide-creativity.com

Boost Children's Confidence and Self-Esteem through Mindfulness Activities. Cultivating a Growth Mind-set is very important for kid's development. This book contains activities so that they can become more confident at school, with friends and, more importantly, with themselves.

www.worldwide-creativity.com

# How to use this journal

Tip: Use the "Look inside" feature on Amazon to see how it looks like

The content of the book is structured so that each day is different. You will find this page template for each day for **50** days with different quotes. Ask your child to fill in the blanks and color the images as in the pattern shown.

The next page contains a powerful quote for each day. Ask your kid to repeat the quote three times and to color both the images and the quote with the colors she likes. Girls will reflect on their unique abilities, expressing how they feel through color.

The next day will contain mindfulness activities and lessons to empower young girls, encouraging them to always be themselves and to love who they are.

# Sneak Peek
## Day 1...

Day: _____  Date: _____

Today I feel: 😄 🙂 😐 🙁 😣

Today I am grateful for:
_____

Something or someone that made me smile/laugh today:
_____

Today I learned:
_____

Today's act of kindness was:
_____

The best part of my day was:
_____

Write or draw something that makes you happy:

**Today is a great day to learn something new**

## Day 2...

Day: _____  Date: _____

Today I feel: 😄 🙂 😐 🙁 😣

Today I am grateful for:
_____

Something or someone that made me smile/laugh today:
_____

Today I learned:
_____

Today's act of kindness was:
_____

The best part of my day was:
_____

Write or draw something that makes you happy:

### ☆ Be kind ☆

Hey there! Being kind often requires courage and strength. What is kindness? Kindness is defined as the quality of being friendly, generous, and considerate. A kind word, a smile, or opening a door can all be acts of kindness. What are some acts of kindness?: clear up a mess you didn't make, use your pocket money to buy a nice new pen for your teacher, clear out your old books and donate them to the school library, offer to play with someone who's all on their own, clear the table after dinner without being asked, draw your mum or dad a picture, just because you love them, make your brother or sister's bed for them, smile and say hello to people you pass on the way to and from school, etc. Kindness includes being kind to yourself. Do you treat yourself kindly? Do you speak gently and kindly to yourself and take good care of yourself?

# A message to you....

Hey there! I want you to know that this journal was born out of passion, from the desire to make things better, and for helping you to grow strong, mindful, and confident. I truly believe that this workbook is a powerful guide, offering you all the necessary tools to achieve that.

With love,

Worldwide Creativity

This journal belongs to an amazing girl! And guess what!?

# THAT GIRL IS YOU !!!

# ALL ABOUT

## I AM ⬡ YEARS OLD ✰

My Friends Are

I live in

I am...

I am...

I am...

I like to watch

Favorite Activities

BOOKS

## FACTS
### About me

My Birthday is:
_____

I am in this grade:
_____

The members of my family:
_____
_____
_____
_____

## My Favorite

Color: _____

Animal: _____

Food: _____

When I grow up I want to be:

*"You are amazing just the way you are!"*

**Day:**_____          **Date:**_____

**Today I feel:** 😄  🙂  😐  🙁  😠

**Today I am grateful for:**

_____

_____

**Something or someone that made me smile/laugh today:**

_____

**Today I learned:**

_____

_____

**Today's act of kindness was:**

_____

**The best part of my day was:**

_____

_____

_____

**Write or draw something that makes you happy:**

# Be Focused

## What you choose to focus on, will grow.

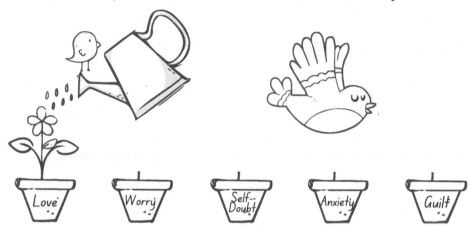

Love | Worry | Self-Doubt | Anxiety | Guilt

Someone used to say: "What you think, you created. What you feel, you attract. What you imagine, you become". So, to understand better, what you put your concentration on, will grow. The reason for this is simply because you are placing your resources in the given area. As a result, this area will grow. Wouldn't be extremely valuable to understand that what you focus on will grow? That's amazing! When you place your attention on something, it will grow. This can be a great thing in terms of creating a high-quality life.

Let's go through a few examples:

- Placing your attention on learning at school will grow your results/grades.
- Placing your attention on mindfulness will grow the skill of mindfulness.
- Placing your attention on your relationships will grow your relationships.

*"Keep looking up, there may be a rainbow waiting for you!"*

Day:_____      Date:_____

Today I feel: 😄 🙂 😐 🙁 😠

Today I am grateful for:

_____

_____

_____

Something or someone that made me smile/laugh today:

_____

Today I learned:

_____

_____

Today's act of kindness was:

_____

The best part of my day was:

_____

_____

_____

Write or draw something that makes you happy:

# Today I shall behave as if this is the day I will be remembered.

-DR. SEUSS-

Wow! This quote is a wonderful reminder that shows us that every day is important and that we should act as if everything we want to accomplish in our lives has already happened.

*"Mistakes are proof that you are trying"*

Day:_____          Date:_____

Today I feel: 😄  🙂  😐  🙁  😠

Today I am grateful for:

_____

_____

_____

Something or someone that made me smile/laugh today:

_____

Today I learned:

_____

_____

Today's act of kindness was:

_____

The best part of my day was:

_____

_____

_____

Write or draw something that makes you happy:

# THE Mindful Jar

The Mindful Jar is a powerful tool that can help you make better choices. Everyone can benefit from improving their positive thinking skills! The idea is that by changing your thinking, you can control your emotions and your actions. Positive thinking skills often start with positive self-talk, which means using the voice in your head to say positive thoughts about yourself or a situation. By beginning to think more positively, you can learn to believe in yourself and work towards your individual potentials.

Instructions: Use a jar that will become your special jar, then think about all the qualities you already have but also those you want to possess. Get some pieces of paper and write down these statements as you repeat them three times. After that, put each piece of paper into the jar to stay there forever so that every time you see it, you will remember what an amazing girl you are.

I am funny
I am happy
I am blessed
I am loved
I am beautiful
I am healthy
I am creative
The Mindful Jar
I am smart
I am amazing
I am kind

*"Don't be afraid to be yourself"*

**Day:**_____ **Date:**_____

Today I feel: 😄 🙂 😐 🙁 😣

Today I am grateful for:

_____

_____

_____

Something or someone that made me smile/laugh today:

_____

Today I learned:

_____

_____

Today's act of kindness was:

_____

The best part of my day was:

_____

_____

_____

Write or draw something that makes you happy:

You're off to great places. Today is your day. Your mountain is waiting so get on your way

-DR. SEUSS-

Yes! Today you have courage! Courage to keep going, courage to find a different way, and of course the courage to try in the first place.

*"To live a creative life, we must lose our fear of being wrong"*

Day:_____          Date:_____

Today I feel: 😄  🙂  😐  🙁  😠

Today I am grateful for:

_____

_____

_____

Something or someone that made me smile/laugh today:

_____

Today I learned:

_____

_____

Today's act of kindness was:

_____

The best part of my day was:

_____

_____

_____

Write or draw something that makes you happy:

# Be Brave

Someone used to say: "Twinkle twinkle little star, BRAVE and BEAUTIFUL is what you are". Courage isn't about something magical that happens inside us to make us "not scared". It's about something magical that happens inside us to make us push through fear and self-doubt and do the things that feel hard or frightening. Courage is being afraid of something and doing it anyway. This can apply to all aspects of life from holding a snake, to telling the truth, to standing up for yourself. Sometimes, courage only has to happen for seconds at a time – just long enough to be brave enough.

*"What makes you different is what makes you beautiful"*

Day:_____          Date:_____

Today I feel: 😄  🙂  😐  🙁  😠

Today I am grateful for:

_____

_____

_____

Something or someone that made me smile/laugh today:

_____

Today I learned:

_____

_____

Today's act of kindness was:

_____

The best part of my day was:

_____

_____

_____

Write or draw something that makes you happy:

# Why fit in when you were born to stand out?

-DR. SEUSS-

So, why be normal when you can be exceptional?! Every day we have the choice to stand out. Every day we have the choice to focus on being amazing, to be exceptional. I am talking about standing out by being yourself, by being extra kind and compassionate toward others. Be proud to stand out! Be confident to stand up for what is right, even when you are the only one doing it.

*"We all have to face the choice between what is right and what is easy"*

Day:_____          Date:_____

Today I feel: 😄   🙂   😐   🙁   😠

Today I am grateful for:

_____

_____

_____

Something or someone that made me smile/laugh today:

_____

Today I learned:

_____

_____

Today's act of kindness was:

_____

The best part of my day was:

_____

_____

_____

Write or draw something that makes you happy:

# ☆Be Open-Minded☆

Hey there! Being open-minded is amazing! To be open-minded is to understand that we are all different and to embrace these differences. It also means being open to new possibilities and adventures. Open-mindedness gives you the ability to embrace different points of view, the ability to be fair, and build trust with others, to be eager to learn new things even if it's challenging, to be an effective team player, etc. Also, an open-minded person embraces the present and appreciates all of the beautiful moments as they unfold.

*"You're braver than you believe, stronger than you seem, and smarter than you think"*

Day:_____          Date:_____

Today I feel: 😄  🙂  😐  😟  😠

Today I am grateful for:

_____

_____

_____

Something or someone that made me smile/laugh today:

_____

Today I learned:

_____

_____

Today's act of kindness was:

_____

The best part of my day was:

_____

_____

_____

Write or draw something that makes you happy:

Today you are you. That is truer than true. There is no one alive who is you-er than you!

-DR. SEUSS-

Be different! Be unique! Be you! We all have our own ways, dreams, and passions that drive us to chase a certain goal in life. Be focused and chase your own path.

*"Be kind, be brave, be creative, be grateful, be happy, be you!"*

Day:_____     Date:_____

Today I feel: 😄  🙂  😐  🙁  😠

Today I am grateful for:

_____

_____

_____

Something or someone that made me smile/laugh today:

_____

Today I learned:

_____

_____

Today's act of kindness was:

_____

The best part of my day was:

_____

_____

_____

Write or draw something that makes you happy:

# Be kind

Hey there! Being kind often requires courage and strength. What is kindness? Kindness is defined as the quality of being friendly, generous, and considerate. A kind word, a smile, or opening a door can all be acts of kindness. What are some acts of kindness? clear up a mess you didn't make, use your pocket money to buy a nice new pen for your teacher, clear out your old books and donate them to the school library, offer to play with someone who's all on their own, clear the table after dinner without being asked, draw your mum or dad a picture, just because you love them, make your brother or sister's bed for them, smile and say hello to people you pass on the way to and from school, etc. Kindness includes being kind to yourself. Do you treat yourself kindly? Do you speak gently and kindly to yourself and take good care of yourself?

*"The more that you read, the more things you will know, the more that you learn, the more places you'll go"*

Day:_____          Date:_____

Today I feel: 😄  🙂  😐  🙁  😠

Today I am grateful for:

_____

_____

Something or someone that made me smile/laugh today:

_____

Today I learned:

_____

_____

Today's act of kindness was:

_____

The best part of my day was:

_____

_____

_____

Write or draw something that makes you happy:

# Today was good, today was fun, tomorrow is another one

-DR. SEUSS-

Live in the present moment. Enjoy each day because tomorrow will be another one. Live in the moment and enjoy what's happening now because the only important moment is the present moment!

*"No one is you, and that is your superpower!"*

Day:_____     Date:_____

Today I feel:  😄  🙂  😐  😟  😠

Today I am grateful for:

_____

_____

_____

Something or someone that made me smile/laugh today:

_____

Today I learned:

_____

_____

Today's act of kindness was:

_____

The best part of my day was:

_____

_____

_____

Write or draw something that makes you happy:

# I am in control

"Even though I may not have control over a situation, I do have control over":

**MY ACTIONS**

**MY WORDS**

**MY THOUGHTS**

**MY EFFORT**

**ASKING FOR HELP**

**MY RESPONSE**

**How I handle my feelings**

*"Always believe that something wonderful is about to happen"*

Day:_____          Date:_____

Today I feel: 😄  🙂  😐  🙁  😠

Today I am grateful for:

_____

_____

_____

Something or someone that made me smile/laugh today:

_____

Today I learned:

_____

_____

Today's act of kindness was:

_____

The best part of my day was:

_____

_____

_____

Write or draw something that makes you happy:

# Things may happen and often they do to people as brainy and footsy as you

-DR. SEUSS

Be persistent in pursuing your dreams, take action, and believe in your dreams. Things will happen, sooner or later.

*"It doesn't matter how slowly you go so long as you do not stop"*

Day:_____          Date:_____

Today I feel: 😄  🙂  😐  😟  😠

Today I am grateful for:

_____

_____

Something or someone that made me smile/laugh today:

_____

Today I learned:

_____

_____

Today's act of kindness was:

_____

The best part of my day was:

_____

_____

_____

Write or draw something that makes you happy:

# Breathe

Practicing breathing exercises can help you to feel calm and safe even when there's a lot going on. Deep breathing has a physical effect on your body and helps you calm down and lower stress. Have you noticed when you inhale a big, slow breath, that you actually feel calmer and more relaxed?

So here is a well-known breathing exercise. This exercise is called "Square Breathing". Follow the instructions below:

- Start at the bottom right of the square
- Breathe in for four counts as you trace the first side of the square
- Hold your breath for four counts as you trace the second side of the square
- Breathe out for four counts as you trace the third side of the square
- Hold your breath for four counts as you trace the final side of the square
- You just completed one deep breath!

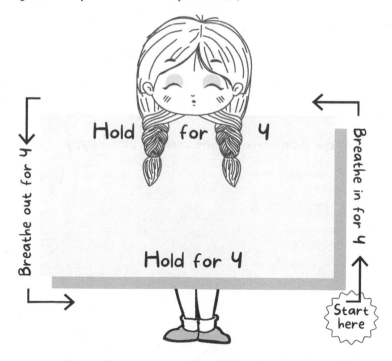

Day:_____          Date:_____

Today I feel: 😄  🙂  😐  🙁  😠

Today I am grateful for:

_____

_____

_____

Something or someone that made me smile/laugh today:

_____

Today I learned:

_____

_____

Today's act of kindness was:

_____

The best part of my day was:

_____

_____

_____

Write or draw something that makes you happy:

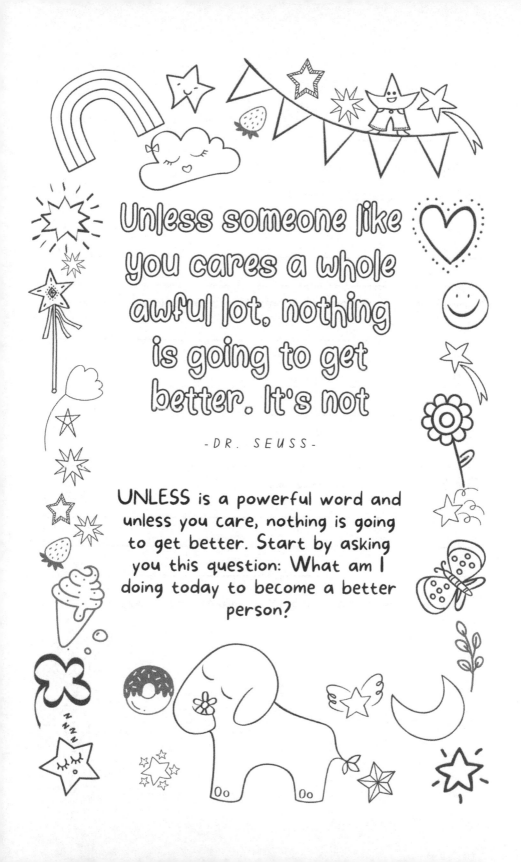

Unless someone like you cares a whole awful lot, nothing is going to get better. It's not

-DR. SEUSS-

UNLESS is a powerful word and unless you care, nothing is going to get better. Start by asking you this question: What am I doing today to become a better person?

*"Kindness is a gift everyone can afford to give"*

Day:_____ Date:_____

Today I feel: 😄 🙂 😐 🙁 😠

Today I am grateful for:

_____
_____
_____

Something or someone that made me smile/laugh today:

_____

Today I learned:

_____
_____

Today's act of kindness was:

_____

The best part of my day was:

_____
_____
_____

Write or draw something that makes you happy:

# An Attitude of Gratitude

Did you know that adopting an attitude of gratitude helps you become happier? It also helps you to become more engaged in your schoolwork and hobbies, and have better grades, and also you can become less anxious, envious, and even depressed, and last but not least, studies show that grateful people tend to sleep better and even live longer. So, what you're thankful for today?

## Today I'm thankful for...

_____

_____

_____

_____

*"A person who never made a mistake never tried anything new"*

Day:_____          Date:_____

Today I feel: 😄  🙂  😐  🙁  😠

Today I am grateful for:

_____

_____

_____

Something or someone that made me smile/laugh today:

_____

Today I learned:

_____

_____

Today's act of kindness was:

_____

The best part of my day was:

_____

_____

_____

Write or draw something that makes you happy:

# From there to here, from here to there, funny things are everywhere

-DR. SEUSS-

This is a powerful reminder that we have to see the beauty in everything. It is up to us how we react to everything that's happening in our lives, so why not choose to see the less good things in a funny way?

*"You don't need a cape to be a hero. You just need to care"*

Day:_____          Date:_____

Today I feel: 😄   🙂   😐   🙁   😠

Today I am grateful for:

_____

_____

_____

Something or someone that made me smile/laugh today:

_____

Today I learned:

_____

_____

Today's act of kindness was:

_____

The best part of my day was:

_____

_____

_____

Write or draw something that makes you happy:

# Be Magical! Be Free!

# Reading is Dreaming with Open Eyes

*"Winners are not people who never fail, but people who never quit"*

Day:_____     Date:_____

Today I feel: 😄  🙂  😐  🙁  😠

Today I am grateful for:

_____
_____

Something or someone that made me smile/laugh today:

_____

Today I learned:

_____
_____

Today's act of kindness was:

_____

The best part of my day was:

_____
_____
_____

Write or draw something that makes you happy:

# Don't cry because it's over, smile because it happened

-DR. SEUSS-

How wonderful is that statement!? Rather than be upset that the holiday is over, we can remember every beautiful moment we had and enjoy it to the maximum.

*"Just in case no one has told you today, you are amazing! Have a really great day!"*

Day: _____          Date: _____

Today I feel: 😄  🙂  😐  🙁  😠

Today I am grateful for:

_____

_____

_____

Something or someone that made me smile/laugh today:

_____

Today I learned:

_____

_____

Today's act of kindness was:

_____

The best part of my day was:

_____

_____

_____

Write or draw something that makes you happy:

Without sadness, there can be no happiness

Everyone wants
HAPPINESS
No one wants
PAIN
But you can't have a
RAINBOW
Without a little
RAIN

*"Happiness can be found even in the darkest of times if one only remembers to turn on the light"*

Day:_____          Date:_____

Today I feel: 😄  🙂  😐  🙁  😠

Today I am grateful for:

_____

_____

_____

Something or someone that made me smile/laugh today:

_____

Today I learned:

_____

_____

Today's act of kindness was:

_____

The best part of my day was:

_____

_____

_____

Write or draw something that makes you happy:

You'll never be bored when you try something new. There's really no limit to what you can do

-DR. SEUSS-

This is a strong reminder that we are limitless and if we think about it, take action and believe, we can do anything!

*"If you see someone without a smile give them one of yours"*

Day:_____          Date:_____

Today I feel:  😄   🙂   😐   🙁   😠

Today I am grateful for:

_____

_____

_____

Something or someone that made me smile/laugh today:

_____

Today I learned:

_____

_____

Today's act of kindness was:

_____

The best part of my day was:

_____

_____

_____

Write or draw something that makes you happy:

# Trace and Breathe

Hey there! Trace along the rainbow with your finger as you breathe in and out.
Wonderful news! This activity uses all five senses (see, touch, hear, smell, taste). While you're breathing in and out (following the lines of the rainbow), think and focus on the things you can see, touch, hear, smell, and taste.

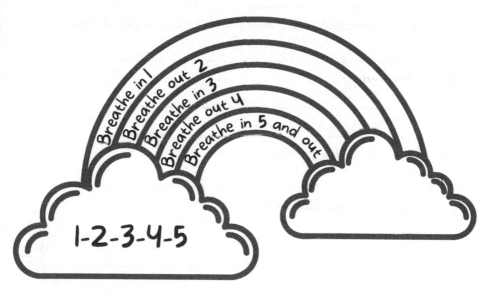

Breathe in 1
Breathe out 2
Breathe in 3
Breathe out 4
Breathe in 5 and out

1-2-3-4-5

one thing you can see:_____

one thing you can touch:_____

one thing you can hear:_____

one thing you can smell:_____

one thing you can taste:_____

Day:_____          Date:_____

Today I feel: 😄  🙂  😐  😟  😠

Today I am grateful for:

_____

_____

_____

Something or someone that made me smile/laugh today:

_____

Today I learned:

_____

Today's act of kindness was:

_____

The best part of my day was:

_____

_____

_____

Write or draw something that makes you happy:

Don't give up! I believe in you all! A person's a person no matter how small!

-DR. SEUSS-

Be confident! Be strong! You are very loved and supported!

*"Do the right thing even when no one is looking"*

Day:_____

Date:_____

Today I feel: 😄 🙂 😐 😟 😠

Today I am grateful for:

_____

_____

_____

Something or someone that made me smile/laugh today:

_____

Today I learned:

_____

_____

Today's act of kindness was:

_____

The best part of my day was:

_____

_____

_____

Write or draw something that makes you happy:

# The Benefits of
## Mindful Breathing

- Helps you feel more calm, relaxed, peaceful and capable;

- Decreases stress, anxiety and tension;

- Keeps the mind and body healthy;

- Lowers your blood pressure and heart rate;

- Helps you sleep better;

- Increases energy level;

- Improves posture;

- Helps to control your emotions;

- Sharpens the ability to focus and learn;

- Promotes appropriate social behaviors;

*"It's not how many times you get knocked down, it's how many times you get back up"*

Day:_____     Date:_____

Today I feel: 😄  🙂  😐  🙁  😠

Today I am grateful for:

_____

_____

_____

Something or someone that made me smile/laugh today:

_____

Today I learned:

_____

_____

Today's act of kindness was:

_____

The best part of my day was:

_____

_____

_____

Write or draw something that makes you happy:

Think left and think right and think low and think high. Oh, the things you can think up if only you try

-DR. SEUSS-

*"Do the best you can until you know better.
Then when you know better, do better"*

Day:_____   Date:_____

Today I feel: 😄  🙂  😐  😟  😠

Today I am grateful for:

_____
_____

Something or someone that made me smile/laugh today:

_____

Today I learned:

_____
_____

Today's act of kindness was:

_____

The best part of my day was:

_____
_____

Write or draw something that makes you happy:

# All About Me

## FUTURE EDITION

Write a letter to your future self from your current self. List the hopes and dreams you'd like to achieve.

Dear _____

_____

_____

_____

_____

_____

_____

_____

_____

_____

_____

_____

From _____

*"Self confidence is a superpower. Once you start to believe in yourself, magic starts happening"*

Day:_____                          Date:_____

Today I feel: 😄  🙂  😐  🙁  😠

Today I am grateful for:

_____

_____

_____

Something or someone that made me smile/laugh today:

_____

Today I learned:

_____

_____

Today's act of kindness was:

_____

The best part of my day was:

_____

_____

_____

Write or draw something that makes you happy:

The expert
in anything
was once
a beginner

-Helen Hayes-

*"It doesn't matter what others are doing. It matters what you are doing"*

Day:_____          Date:_____

Today I feel: 😄  🙂  😐  🙁  😠

Today I am grateful for:

_____

_____

_____

Something or someone that made me smile/laugh today:

_____

Today I learned:

_____

_____

Today's act of kindness was:

_____

The best part of my day was:

_____

_____

_____

Write or draw something that makes you happy:

Be Happy!

Be so HAPPY that when others

Look at YOU they become HAPPY too

Today I'm happy because...

_____

_____

_____

*"What you do today can improve all your tomorrows"*

Day:_____ Date:_____

Today I feel: 😄 🙂 😐 🙁 😠

Today I am grateful for:

_____
_____
_____

Something or someone that made me smile/laugh today:

_____

Today I learned:

_____
_____

Today's act of kindness was:

_____

The best part of my day was:

_____
_____
_____

Write or draw something that makes you happy:

I know it is wet
and the sun is
not sunny, but
we can have
lots of good fun
that is funny!

-Dr. Seuss-

Day:_____          Date:_____

Today I feel: 😄  🙂  😐  🙁  😠

Today I am grateful for:

_____

_____

_____

Something or someone that made me smile/laugh today:

_____

Today I learned:

_____

_____

Today's act of kindness was:

_____

The best part of my day was:

_____

_____

_____

Write or draw something that makes you happy:

# Be Kind!

## PRACTICE
### simple acts of
### kindness
### ♡ every day ♡

Acts of kindness I made this week...

_____
_____
_____
_____

*"No act of kindness, no matter how small, is ever wasted"*

Day:_____     Date:_____

Today I feel: 😄  🙂  😐  😟  😠

Today I am grateful for:

_____

_____

Something or someone that made me smile/laugh today:

_____

Today I learned:

_____

_____

Today's act of kindness was:

_____

The best part of my day was:

_____

_____

_____

Write or draw something that makes you happy:

All things
are difficult
before they
are easy

-Thomas Fuller-

*"By being yourself, you put something wonderful in the world that was not there before"*

Day:_____          Date:_____

Today I feel: 😄   🙂   😐   😟   😠

Today I am grateful for:

_____

_____

_____

Something or someone that made me smile/laugh today:

_____

Today I learned:

_____

_____

Today's act of kindness was:

_____

The best part of my day was:

_____

_____

_____

Write or draw something that makes you happy:

Shoot for the moon. Even if you miss, you'll land among the stars

-Norman Vincent-

*"Attitude is a little thing that makes a big difference"*

Day:_____ Date:_____

Today I feel: 😄 🙂 😐 🙁 😠

Today I am grateful for:

_____

_____

_____

Something or someone that made me smile/laugh today:

_____

Today I learned:

_____

_____

Today's act of kindness was:

_____

The best part of my day was:

_____

_____

_____

Write or draw something that makes you happy:

# Things to do when you're upset

Tell yourself to calm down. Slowly repeat phrases to yourself like "take it easy", "it will pass" or whatever works for you.

Take time out. Take a walk or go for a run.

Use visualization to calm down. Close your eyes and picture yourself in your favorite place.

Slow down and focus on your breathing. Take deep breaths in through your nose, and slowly out through your mouth.

Try to replace negative thoughts with positive ones. Even if you're feeling upset, remind yourself that getting angry isn't going to fix the way that you're feeling.

Start reading your favorite book, or favorite chapter

Day:_____          Date:_____

Today I feel: 😄  🙂  😐  🙁  😠

Today I am grateful for:

_____

_____

_____

Something or someone that made me smile/laugh today:

_____

Today I learned:

_____

Today's act of kindness was:

_____

The best part of my day was:

_____

_____

_____

Write or draw something that makes you happy:

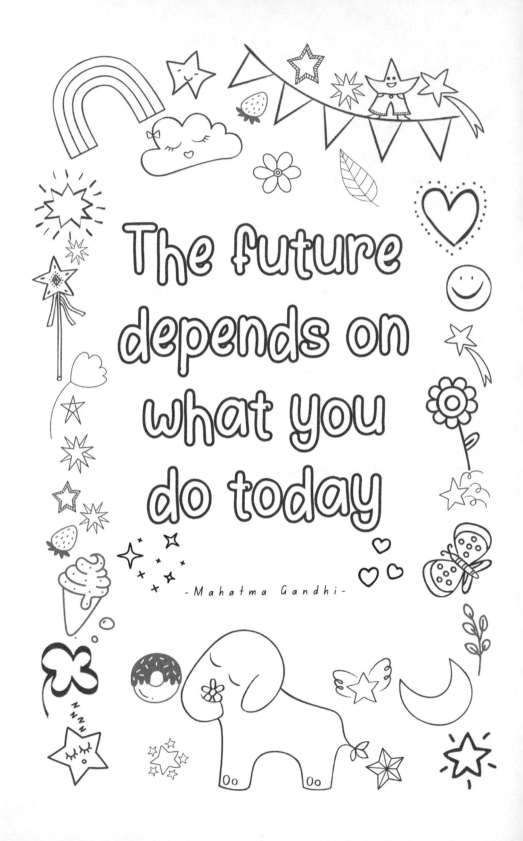

The future depends on what you do today

-Mahatma Gandhi-

*"Think positive and positive things will happen"*

Day:_____          Date:_____

Today I feel: 😄  🙂  😐  🙁  😠

Today I am grateful for:

_____
_____
_____

Something or someone that made me smile/laugh today:

_____

Today I learned:

_____
_____

Today's act of kindness was:

_____

The best part of my day was:

_____
_____
_____

Write or draw something that makes you happy:

# 10 Ways to show KINDNESS

Forgive someone for a mistake

**1**

Let someone else first

**2**

Do an extra chore

**3**

Help clean up

**4**

Give someone a high-five

**5**

Write someone a kind note

**6**

Hold the door open for others

**7**

Encourage a friend

**8**

Donate old books

**9**

Invite someone to join you

**10**

Day:_____      Date:_____

Today I feel: 😄  🙂  😐  😟  😠

Today I am grateful for:

_____

_____

_____

Something or someone that made me smile/laugh today:

_____

Today I learned:

_____

_____

Today's act of kindness was:

_____

The best part of my day was:

_____

_____

_____

Write or draw something that makes you happy:

*Never say "I can't". Always say "I'll try"*

Day:_____          Date:_____

Today I feel: 😄   🙂   😐   🙁   😠

Today I am grateful for:

_____

_____

_____

Something or someone that made me smile/laugh today:

_____

Today I learned:

_____

_____

Today's act of kindness was:

_____

The best part of my day was:

_____

_____

_____

Write or draw something that makes you happy:

# THINK

Before you speak, make sure that...

**T** is it **TRUE**

**H** is it **HELPFUL**

**I** is it **INSPIRING**

**N** is it **NECESSARY**

**K** is it **KIND**

Day:_____          Date:_____

Today I feel: 😄  🙂  😐  🙁  😠

Today I am grateful for:
_____
_____
_____

Something or someone that made me smile/laugh today:
_____

Today I learned:
_____
_____

Today's act of kindness was:
_____

The best part of my day was:
_____
_____
_____

Write or draw something that makes you happy:

*"Faith in your soul, hope in your mind, love on your heart"*

Day:_____     Date:_____

Today I feel: 😄  🙂  😐  🙁  😠

Today I am grateful for:

_____

_____

_____

Something or someone that made me smile/laugh today:

_____

Today I learned:

_____

_____

Today's act of kindness was:

_____

The best part of my day was:

_____

_____

_____

Write or draw something that makes you happy:

# What to tell myself when I'm feeling
## DISCOURAGED

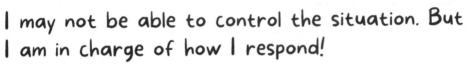

This is tough. But so am I!

I may not be able to control the situation. But I am in charge of how I respond!

I haven't figured this out...yet

This challenge is here to teach me something.

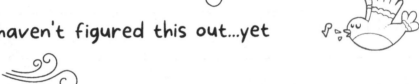

All I need to do is take it one step at a time. Breathe and do the next right thing.

*"A smile is the best makeup any girl can wear"*

Day:_____          Date:_____

Today I feel: 😄  ☺  😐  😟  😠

Today I am grateful for:

_____

_____

_____

Something or someone that made me smile/laugh today:

_____

Today I learned:

_____

_____

Today's act of kindness was:

_____

The best part of my day was:

_____

_____

_____

Write or draw something that makes you happy:

*"We can choose to be grateful no matter what"*

Day:_____

Date:_____

Today I feel: 😄  🙂  😐  🙁  😠

Today I am grateful for:

_____

_____

_____

Something or someone that made me smile/laugh today:

_____

Today I learned:

_____

_____

Today's act of kindness was:

_____

The best part of my day was:

_____

_____

_____

Write or draw something that makes you happy:

# Gratitude
# P R O M P T S

A quality of mine for which I am grateful is:

_____

Something that makes me smile/laugh for which I'm grateful is:

_____

Something in nature that I'm grateful for is:

_____

A beautiful memory I'm grateful for is:

_____

A challenge I'm grateful for is:

_____

A friend I'm grateful for is:

_____

A teacher I'm grateful for is:

_____

A game I'm grateful for is:

_____

A book I'm grateful for is:

_____

Day:_____                    Date:_____

Today I feel:  😄   🙂   😐   😟   😠

Today I am grateful for:

_____

_____

_____

Something or someone that made me smile/laugh today:

_____

Today I learned:

_____

_____

Today's act of kindness was:

_____

The best part of my day was:

_____

_____

_____

Write or draw something that makes you happy:

*"Believe you can and you're halfway there"*

Day:_____ Date:_____

Today I feel: 😄  🙂  😐  🙁  😠

Today I am grateful for:

_____

_____

_____

Something or someone that made me smile/laugh today:

_____

Today I learned:

_____

_____

Today's act of kindness was:

_____

The best part of my day was:

_____

_____

_____

Write or draw something that makes you happy:

# "This challenge is teaching me"

Challenges are important parts of life that give you experiences, make you learn and help you to become wiser and stronger. Challenges make you grow and shape you.

Remember a challenge you had and what it taught you, then tick the box next to the correct answers.

- [ ] that I am brave
- [ ] how to be more flexible
- [ ] how to take better care of my feelings
- [ ] how to be more responsible
- [ ] that I am still lovable and important, no matter what
- [ ] how to find solutions
- [ ] I am stronger that I realized
- [ ] I may not be able to control the situation but I can choose how to respond to it

*"Dream until your dreams come true"*

Day:_____          Date:_____

Today I feel: 😄  🙂  😐  🙁  😠

Today I am grateful for:
_____
_____
_____

Something or someone that made me smile/laugh today:
_____

Today I learned:
_____
_____

Today's act of kindness was:
_____

The best part of my day was:
_____
_____
_____

Write or draw something that makes you happy:

*"Dream higher than the sky, deeper than the ocean"*

Day:_____          Date:_____

Today I feel: 😄  🙂  😐  🙁  😠

Today I am grateful for:

_____
_____
_____

Something or someone that made me smile/laugh today:

_____

Today I learned:

_____
_____

Today's act of kindness was:

_____

The best part of my day was:

_____
_____
_____

Write or draw something that makes you happy:

# Be a Self-Coach
## Have a healthy self-talk

| Say this | Instead of this |
|---|---|
| Whoops. I made a mistake | I'm so dumb |
| I like me | No one likes me |
| I did something bad | I'm a bad person |
| This is really hard but I'm going to keep trying | I give up. I'll never be able to do this |
| I haven't figured it out...yet | I never get anything right |
| I am enough, worthy and important | I'm not good enough |

*"The best things in life are the people we love, the places we've been, and the memories we've made along the way"*

Day:_____          Date:_____

Today I feel: 😄   🙂   😐   😟   😠

Today I am grateful for:
_____
_____
_____

Something or someone that made me smile/laugh today:
_____

Today I learned:
_____
_____

Today's act of kindness was:
_____

The best part of my day was:
_____
_____
_____

Write or draw something that makes you happy:

*"The meaning of life is to find your gift. The purpose of life is to give it away"*

Day:_____          Date:_____

Today I feel: 😄  🙂  😐  🙁  😠

Today I am grateful for:

_____

_____

_____

Something or someone that made me smile/laugh today:

_____

Today I learned:

_____

_____

Today's act of kindness was:

_____

The best part of my day was:

_____

_____

_____

Write or draw something that makes you happy:

 # A worry is...

A worry can be a thought or an idea that describes different feelings and makes you feel upset, tired, uncomfortable, nervous, or even frustrated.

It is very important to realize first of all what thoughts or ideas trigger these states. When you're done with that, make a list of all your worries and fears. Just the act of recognizing and writing down worries can sometimes make the scary emotions seem less intimidating. So, let's start making this list below.

_____

_____

_____

_____

_____

_____

_____

_____

"Always believe that something wonderful is about to happen"

Day:_____          Date:_____

Today I feel: 😄  🙂  😐  🙁  😠

Today I am grateful for:

_____

_____

_____

Something or someone that made me smile/laugh today:

_____

Today I learned:

_____

_____

Today's act of kindness was:

_____

The best part of my day was:

_____

_____

_____

Write or draw something that makes you happy:

Day:_____     Date:_____

Today I feel: 😄  🙂  😐  🙁  😠

Today I am grateful for:

_____

_____

_____

Something or someone that made me smile/laugh today:

_____

Today I learned:

_____

_____

Today's act of kindness was:

_____

The best part of my day was:

_____

_____

_____

Write or draw something that makes you happy:

# Mindful Mantras

One way to have a mindful moment is to form a mantra. A mantra is a phrase that you can say in your mind or even out loud, which makes you feel much better no matter the situation. For example: "I am creative and I can do hard things"

*To complete mantras, use words from the list below*

beautiful

generous

healthy

calm

kind

loving

peaceful

strong

brave

Today will be a _____ day and I'll do my best to keep it like that.

May I be _____ and _____. May you be _____ and _____.

I will be _____ and _____ to everyone I meet today.

I will smile and be _____ as much as I can.

I am _____ and
I am _____ may always be like this.

Day:_____      Date:_____

Today I feel: 😄 🙂 😐 🙁 😠

Today I am grateful for:

_____

_____

_____

Something or someone that made me smile/laugh today:

_____

Today I learned:

_____

_____

Today's act of kindness was:

_____

The best part of my day was:

_____

_____

_____

Write or draw something that makes you happy:

# Thank You

As a small family business, your feedback is very important to us and we will appreciate it if you could take a little time to rate it on Amazon. This will be very helpful for us, the creators of the book, as well as for other people to analyze the quality of the product.

We really hope you enjoy our work and find it really useful for your children.
This book was made with great care so your children can develop mindfulness and gratitude and grow strong and confident.

We create our book with lots of love, but mistakes can always happen. If there are any issues with your book such as faulty bindings or printing errors, please contact the platform you purchased to obtain a replacement.

contact@worldwide-creativity.com

WC Worldwide Creativity
Mindfulness

Can't wait to see you on **Instagram**

**Instagram** https://www.instagram.com/worldwidecreativitypress/

Qr-code

Can't wait to see you on **Facebook**

**Facebook** https://www.facebook.com/worldwidecreativitypress/

Qr-code

Visit our **Website**

**Website** https://worldwide-creativity.com/

Qr-code

Made in the USA
Middletown, DE
31 May 2023

31784727R00064